The Nativity Story for Kids

The Birth of Jesus Christ

Written by Andrea Clarke Pratt

Copyright@2022. All rights reserved. Andrea Clarke Pratt

Unless otherwise indicated, Scripture quotations taken from the King James Version (KJV) - public domain.

Dedication

This book is dedicated to my grandson Kingsley.

May he grow to embrace God's love and plan for his life.

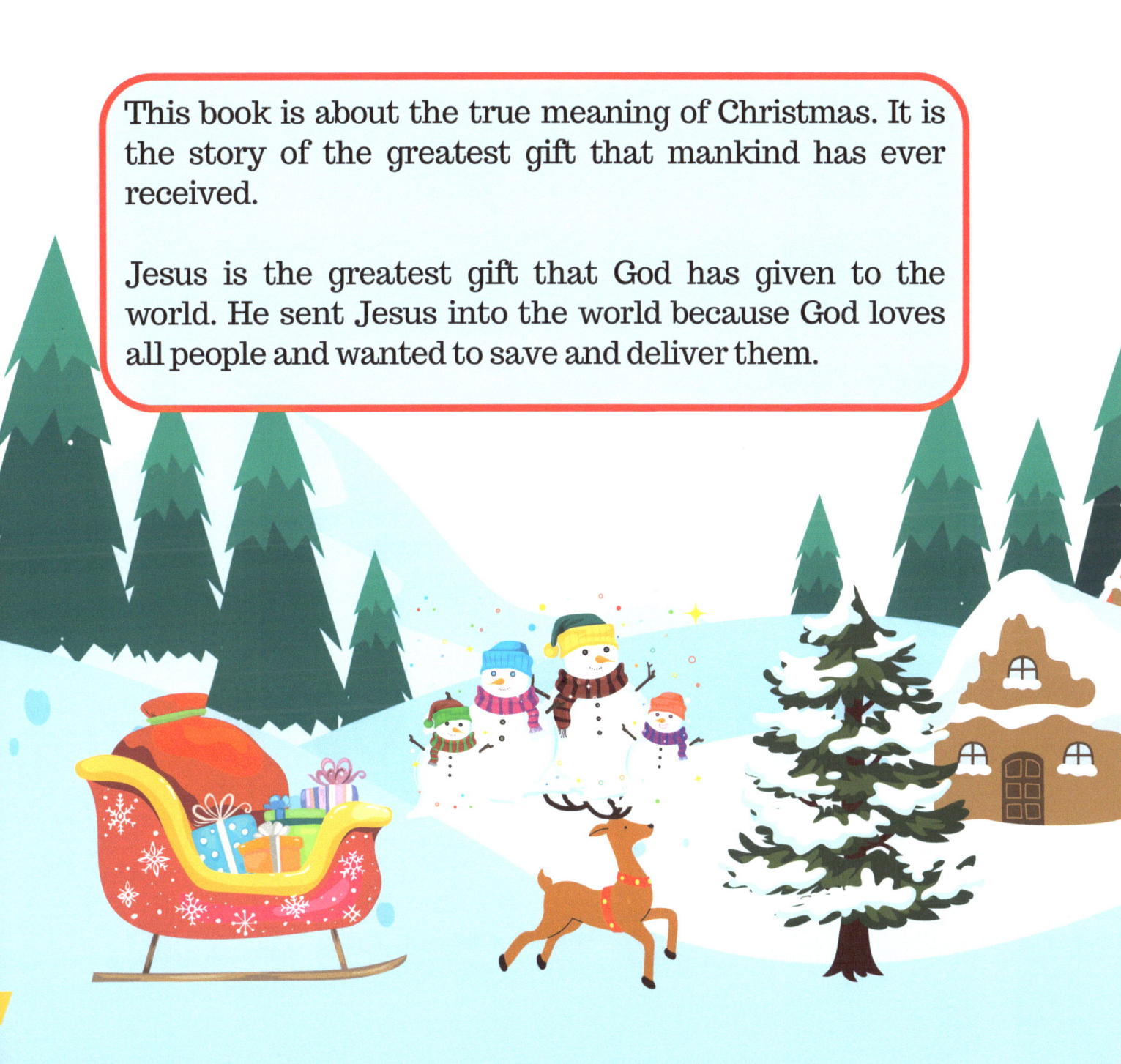

This book is about the true meaning of Christmas. It is the story of the greatest gift that mankind has ever received.

Jesus is the greatest gift that God has given to the world. He sent Jesus into the world because God loves all people and wanted to save and deliver them.

Joseph decided to obey the messenger sent by God and married Mary.

When Mary was almost ready to have the baby, Caesar Augustus decreed that the world be taxed. Joseph and Mary left Nazareth and traveled on a long journey to Bethlehem, Joseph's hometown to be taxed.

When they finally arrived in Bethlehem, there were no rooms available in the inns. There was one place that was available, though: a stable. A stable is a building where animals are fed and cared for.

Baby Jesus, who is also called the Lamb of God, was born in a stable because there was no unoccupied room in the inns. Do you see a lamb in the picture?

JESUS CHRIST WAS BORN

Mary wrapped baby Jesus in swaddling clothes and gently placed him in a manger.

Christmas is celebrated to remember the birth of Jesus.

Most kings were born in beautiful castles, but Jesus, the Savior of the world, was born in a humble stable.

At this time, shepherds were in the field caring for their sheep when an angel appeared and told them the good news of the birth of Jesus.

He told the shepherds they would find the baby wrapped in swaddling clothes in a manger in Bethlehem.

The wise men brought with them gifts of gold, frankincense, and myrrh to present to the baby. When the wise men arrived in Jerusalem, they asked where the King of the Jews had been born because they had seen his star.

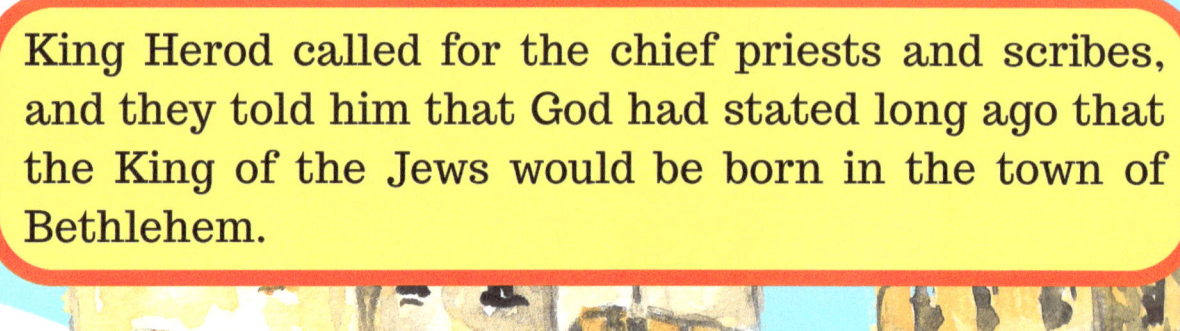

King Herod called for the chief priests and scribes, and they told him that God had stated long ago that the King of the Jews would be born in the town of Bethlehem.

King Herod then told the wise men that the King of the Jews would be born in Bethlehem. He told them that when they find the baby, they should let him know so he could also worship him. But Herod only really wanted to find the baby so he could kill him.

At first, Mary did not fully understand God's plans, but she accepted them and was obedient.

Like Mary, God has great plans for your life. God will do great things in your life too if you accept him.

"But as it is written, Eye hath not seen, nor ear heard, Neither have entered into the heart of man, The things which God hath prepared for them that love him."

1 Corinthians 2:9

www.ingramcontent.com/pod-product-compliance
Lightning Source LLC
LaVergne TN
LVHW070442070526
838199LV00036B/685